First published in the UK by Sweet Cherry Publishing Limited, 2024
Unit 36, Vulcan House, Vulcan Road,
Leicester, LE5 3EF, United Kingdom

Sweet Cherry Europe (Europe address)
Nauschgasse 4/3/2 POB 1017
Vienna, WI 1220, Austria

2 4 6 8 10 9 7 5 3 1

ISBN: 978-1-80263-093-0

Football Rising Stars: Alessia Russo

© Sweet Cherry Publishing Limited, 2024

Text by Harry Meredith
Illustrations by Sophie Jones

All rights reserved. No part of this publication may be reproduced or utilised in any form or by any means, electronic or mechanical, including photocopying, recording, or using any information storage and retrieval system, without prior permission in writing from the publisher.

The right of Harry Meredith to be identified as the author of this work has been asserted by them in accordance with the Copyright, Designs and Patents Act 1988.

www.sweetcherrypublishing.com

Printed and bound in Turkey

ALESSIA RUSSO

THE UNOFFICIAL STORY

Written by
HARRY MEREDITH

CONTENTS

1. The Comeback	7
2. Sicily to Maidstone	17
3. Academy Football	26
4. England Youth	33
5. Decision Time	43
6. North Carolina Tar Heels	52
7. Fourth Year	61
8. Manchester United: The Red Devils	69
9. England Debut	77
10. Euro 2022	85
11. The Russo	95
12. The Final	104
13. The Rumour Mill	117
14. Alessia's Choice	123

1
THE COMEBACK

On the 19th of November 2022, two football teams emerged from the tunnel to the sound of thunderous applause. Over 40,000 fans had come to watch Arsenal play Manchester United at the Emirates Stadium in London. It was a top of the table clash in the Women's Super League, and both sides wanted to continue their impressive early season form and earn first place.

Claiming victory today for either side would set the tone for the remainder of the season. Arsenal were on a fourteen-match unbeaten run, and now they were heading into this match at their home stadium with the majority of the fans in attendance backing them. Manchester United had been playing well too, but they would need to play at their best in order to put a stop to this Arsenal side.

★ ALESSIA RUSSO ★

Playing up front, Manchester United had the commanding Alessia Russo to rely upon. At twenty-three years old, she was far from the most experienced player in the team but she was certainly one of the most talented. She had a knack for scoring goals and today her team needed her. If Alessia was playing at her best then Manchester United had a chance at winning this game.

The opening exchanges in the match were cagey. Both sides pushed to find the first goal, but they were

also scared to concede. It was this fear and pressure that led to the first goal in the match. In the 39th minute, Alessia headed out wide to win the ball and brought it under her control. With defenders surrounding her, Alessia played a neat pass between them to send her teammate Hayley Ladd on a run down the right wing. The midfielder crossed the ball into the box. Arsenal's goalkeeper, Manuela Zinsberger, came to meet it

but ended up flapping at nothing. She missed the ball and it fell to the feet of Ella Toone, who took advantage of the error and cushioned the ball into the net. Toone ran away with a smile, making a heart sign with her hands as she celebrated her goal with her teammates. Manchester United had the lead – but there was still plenty of football left to be played.

Arsenal started the second half with a determination to get back into the game, and it didn't take them long. Frida Maanum darted into the opponent's half and took a shot at goal from distance. Cruelly, the shot hit the leg of Maya Le Tissier, a Manchester United defender, and looped into the goal. Mary Earps in goal was unable to do anything as the back of the net rippled. The game was level again.

Riding on a wave of momentum, Arsenal continued to pile pressure onto their opponents. In the 73rd minute, Katie McCabe sent a curved cross into the box with her left foot. The curling ball evaded all of the defenders and was met with a powerful strike from Laura

★ ALESSIA RUSSO ★

Wienroither. The game had turned entirely on its head. Arsenal, with thousands of fans cheering them on, were now in the lead. Surely they could hold on for the final twenty minutes? That was yet to be decided, as Alessia and her teammates would do everything they could to get back into this game. They pushed and pushed, but the Arsenal defence stood strong. In the 85th minute, Manchester United earned a free kick and the captain, Katie Zelem, fired the ball into the box. A crowd of defenders and attackers were ready to

go for the ball, but it was a Manchester United head that reached it first. Millie Turner headed it towards goal, and Alessia watched as the ball hit the crossbar then bounced over the line. Manchester United had scored a late equaliser and everything was square once more! Each team appeared to be heading home with one point, but was there enough time for one of them to take home even more?

In the 91st minute, Manchester United had a corner. The thousands of Arsenal fans in the stadium were

on the edges of their seats, hoping for a clearance. Zelem crossed the ball into the box and players jostled for position. Alessia rose highest, with defenders trying to put her off, but they could do nothing except watch the ball fly into the net. The away fans in the stadium roared, as did the players. Manchester United had done it! They had a 2–3 lead and were on course to stop Arsenal's seemingly unstoppable run. The final minutes of the match passed by and the referee blew her whistle. Alessia and her team had won, gaining three important points. Once again, their star striker had made her mark in an important match. No matter the circumstance, no matter the score, any team has a chance when Alessia is leading the line.

2
SICILY TO MAIDSTONE

The Russo family's story begins far away from the wet and windy shores of Britain, on the searingly hot Italian island of Sicily. In the 1950s, Alessia's grandfather had opted to swap the sun for the rain, when he chose to move to England in search of a new life filled with opportunity and hope. This eventually led to him starting a family in Maidstone, Kent. And on the 8th of February 1999, Carol and Mario Russo welcomed Alessia Mia Teresa into the world.

Alessia was born into a football mad family, so it was almost inevitable that she would get drawn into the sport. When her grandfather arrived in England, he quickly became a Manchester United fan. This love for football trickled down the family tree to Alessia's father, who became

ALESSIA RUSSO

a non-league footballer for the Metropolitan Police FC – a club where he was the top goalscorer. Her older brothers, Giorgio and Luca, were also football mad. As a young girl, Alessia would watch them play in matches from the touchline. But when no one was looking, she would sneak a ball from the kit bag and start kicking it, dribbling with it and practising all of the cool tricks she'd seen footballers do. By the age of six, it was clear that Alessia wanted to join in. When she wasn't playing with a ball on the touchline, she was playing with one

FOOTBALL RISING STARS

in the family's back garden. Noticing their daughter's desire to play

football, Alessia's parents helped her find a team to join.

They found a local club known as West Farleigh FC. It was a team that consisted almost entirely of boys, but the coach was willing to let girls join too. Having grown up playing football with her brothers, Alessia wasn't fazed at all by the prospect of playing against boys. She immediately got stuck into life at her new team and started to earn

ALESSIA RUSSO

her place. At first, Alessia's preferred position was as a midfielder. There were moments when it wasn't easy, as she was usually the only girl on the pitch, but her love for the sport pulled her through. It also helped that the team welcomed and accepted her. She was treated as one of the club's own by all of the boys and they quickly became friends.

It helped that Alessia clearly possessed a heap of talent too. During crucial moments in matches, the coach would often ask the boys to get the ball to Alessia. They all knew that the team's best chance of winning was to give her as many opportunities as possible.

As well as playing for West Farleigh, Alessia often joined football camps during half-terms or summer holidays. But after some time with West Farleigh, Alessia couldn't help but wonder what it would be like to play in a team made up entirely of girls. She didn't want to leave her  friends at the club behind, but she knew that playing for a girls' team was something she wanted to do. And so, eight-year-old Alessia chose to join Bearsted FC under 9s. She was an immediate hit for the team, and was actually seen as too good to play for her own year group. Instead, Alessia was asked to play with the U10s – a team that might test her ability a little further. She rose to the challenge and embraced it. Even while playing against players older than her, Alessia stood out on the pitch. She played for Bearsted FC for a year, and she overcame every obstacle in her path. It had become apparent that Alessia was an incredible football player who deserved a shot at a higher level.

These were the same thoughts held by professional scouts who had come to watch Alessia play. She displayed a technical ability far beyond her age, and she had a strength and determination that would suit her well in a professional academy setup. After her first year with Bearsted FC, it was time for another move and a tougher challenge. Alessia was offered the chance to play at Charlton

Athletic's Centre of Excellence, swapping weekend matches and sporadic training sessions for organised drills and competitive matches.

3
ACADEMY FOOTBALL

Alessia thrived after making the switch to academy football. It made sense for her to join an academy in London, because it meant that she wouldn't have to travel far from her home. She did have to commute a reasonable distance each week, but her parents found the time in their busy schedules to ensure that Alessia could attend.

Alessia embraced life as an academy footballer. She trained hard, competed in matches and gave her all to improving herself. She even tried her best to feel a part of the club as a whole. For one particular league match, Alessia was a matchday mascot for Charlton Athletic. At the time, the team were competing at the highest level of women's football in England, so being a mascot was a great honour for Alessia. She emerged from the tunnel with Casey Stoney, the team's captain and an established defender who also played regularly for England. As they walked out onto the pitch, Alessia looked around. She smiled at the fans cheering their team on, hoping that one day she would be a player rather than a mascot.

Alessia enjoyed her time at the centre of excellence. She was able to learn from talented coaches, push herself against gifted peers and take her football skills to new heights.

But while Alessia was reaching higher, unfortunately the club was going in the opposite direction. As a result, ten-year-old Alessia was offered the chance to play for Chelsea, a London club that had one of the best academies in the country. Many of the country's top talents learnt their trade at Chelsea's famous Cobham training centre; it was a place where unpolished gems became sought-after jewels.

It was exciting to be given this opportunity, although Alessia couldn't help but feel sad about what was unfolding at Charlton Athletic. In 2007, the men's team were relegated from the Premier League, which meant that the club would lose out on a lot of financial assistance and revenue. A controversial decision was made to disband the entire women's team in order to cut costs. The women's team had done well that year, making it all the way to an FA Cup final, but this hadn't changed anything. Unfortunately, the horrible truth was that there wasn't much money within the women's game

★ ALESSIA RUSSO ★

because not enough people watched it. Not because it lacked importance, but because it wasn't given the same glamour and coverage as the men's game. And so, the women's team's fate was out of their hands. Alessia had to watch as many of her old coaches and favourite players were released by the club, demonstrating to her just how unpredictable the world of women's football can be. But Alessia's ambition hadn't changed. She didn't just want to become a footballer; she wanted to help change women's football.

She wanted to make football a fairer sport where women were given the same opportunities as men.

With her newfound determination, Alessia slotted right into life at Chelsea's academy. She didn't look out of place in a top tier football academy, and this was quickly noticed by many outside of the club. In fact, not too long after joining, the national team came knocking at her door.

4
ENGLAND YOUTH

When Alessia was thirteen, she was called up to play for England. Playing for her country was not entirely new – Alessia had attended a handful of national school camps – but this was her first ever official call-up to an England youth team. Alessia

 could hardly contain her excitement when she found out and immediately told all of her friends and family. She was going to play with the best girls in the country. England had identified Alessia as one of those girls and believed they could help shape and develop her into a future England talent. Perhaps she could even play for the England senior team one day?

With England's youth team, Alessia was able to participate in international tournaments and matches across the world. She travelled to countries not ordinarily found in a travel brochure and experienced many different climates. It was in these matches and tournaments that Alessia made some of her closest friends, quickly creating a support network of people similar to her. Although the girls were competing with one another, they were still going through the same experiences. They had been taken out of their regular teenage lives and put into a pressurised and demanding environment. So, by coming together, they could enjoy their downtime and make trips away feel like a holiday. The group of friends grew up playing football together through the national age groups, and they soon became very close. To this day, Alessia is still part of a group chat called 'Good Peeps', which is made up of the players she met during this time in her life.

While playing internationally for England had plenty of positives, there were also some negatives. Alessia would often have to ask for time off school in order to attend. She was

✦ ALESSIA RUSSO ✦

fine with it, but at first her teachers and school weren't so sure. Alessia had to trudge over to the headmaster's office and frequently ask for eight, nine or even ten days off school. After some convincing, her school were understanding – but they did ask her to meet a number of conditions. Alessia was allowed to play as long as she studied when she could and made sure her time away didn't affect her education. Plus, it helped that the national team provided academic help to all players while they were away.

Alessia tried to impress during her first England camp, and she succeeded. She trained hard and played exceptionally with the country's other top talents. As a result, Alessia was invited back to compete in further camps, representing England for the U15s and U17s.

Alessia was also able to compete in international tournaments. She was included in the 2016 FIFA U17 World Cup, which took place in Jordan. Once they had settled in after

★ ALESSIA RUSSO ★

their arrival, the England team came together to eat and relax at their hotel base. Alessia loved to chat as she ate her food, and she was talking to her friends while eating some pasta. But the pasta somehow became lodged in her throat. She could hardly breathe! One of the club's coaches had to help her clear the blockage, and thankfully she was completely fine. With pasta being an Italian food, Alessia was able to laugh about the irony of the situation with her friends.

England had been drawn against

North Korea, Nigeria and Brazil in a tough group. The first match was against North Korea, and it was a dramatic game filled with chances and goals. The game was approaching its end, with North Korea holding a shock 3-2 lead, but there were still valuable seconds on the clock. In the 94th minute, Alessia fired in a late equaliser that brought the game level. She had earned a deserved point for her side and avoided defeat on the opening day of the competition. England then drew 0-0 against Nigeria, before defeating Brazil 2–1 to earn themselves a spot in the knock-out rounds.

Yet this was where Alessia and England's tournament came to an end. Despite all of their efforts, the team were unable to overcome a strong Japan side in the quarter-finals. They lost the match 3-0, and Japan made it all the way to the final of the competition.

Alessia was a star at academy level and for England. She appeared to be heading in only one direction: to a future in football filled with appearances, goals and awards. But Alessia's football journey was only just beginning and her steady pathway was leading towards a crossroads.

The world of football can often be harsh and unpredictable. Football is like nothing else when you're winning, but it can be a lonely and frustrating sport when times are tough.

5
DECISION TIME

Alessia played at Chelsea's academy for an impressive six years, consistently making the cut year after year while other players were let go. She was a recognised and loyal player who had been given all of the tools to succeed within the world of football. During her time at Chelsea, Alessia was even made development squad captain, because she was seen as a leader on the pitch. While she was a reserved and sometimes shy character off the pitch, Alessia became a commander the moment her boots touched the grass. She always gave her best and expected everyone else to do the same. And after all of those years with Chelsea, it appeared that Alessia was heading towards the next step. It was time for her to take her chance and go from an academy player to a professional footballer. She wanted to play for the Chelsea first team and make her mark in the women's game.

Alessia was brought into the women's team and began to train with the club's stars. The club's players were reaching new heights, competing not only in the Women's Super League, but for European and domestic trophies too. It was in a domestic competition, the League Cup, that Alessia made her debut for Chelsea's first team.

Alessia had played hundreds of times for Chelsea's academy, but her

 first appearance also turned out to be her last for the women's team. Alessia wasn't getting much game time at all, and there were whispers that perhaps she might even be released from the club. But before this happened, Alessia decided to take her fate into her own hands. At seventeen years old, she decided to end her time with Chelsea and embark on the next stage of her football journey, setting out on a pathway that she had chosen for herself.

Alessia had decided what she wanted to do next, but there was

★ ALESSIA RUSSO ★

still some time before she could go out and do it. In the meantime, Alessia decided to continue playing football in England. She joined Brighton & Hove Albion (nicknamed The Seagulls), a team that were competing in the second division of women's football at the time. Alessia played in seven matches and scored three goals during her short stint with the club, giving her a much-needed confidence boost after how things had worked out at Chelsea. Alessia was clearly a talented footballer who deserved her place on the pitch. She could have continued with The Seagulls, but she had another adventure in mind.

Alessia's footballing experience had made her question what she wanted  to do with her life. She had dedicated so much of her time to football that it was terrifying to think about just how quickly that dream could be taken away from her. Alessia felt that she needed a backup, an alternative plan to provide her with an academic education as well as a footballing one.

★ ALESSIA RUSSO ★

She was going to make sure that she had options outside of football, if she wasn't able to make a career out of the sport. So, it was time for a drastic action; it was time to enact the next part of her plan.

Alessia was going to study at university. She wasn't going to study in England, or even Europe, but instead Alessia was going across the pond to the USA – where they mostly refer to universities as colleges. Alessia would be studying at and playing for a prestigious college football team, thousands of miles away from home. The prospect of this excited Alessia, but it was also mixed with a sense of fear and apprehension. She would be leaving behind everyone and everything she knew!

Despite these fears, there was no stopping Alessia. One of her older brothers, Luca, had studied in the US at the University of Missouri on a track and field scholarship, so Alessia relied on his help when sorting out her administrative paperwork. After numerous meetings, including a visit to the US embassy in London, Alessia was granted a visa to study and live in the US throughout her college years.

Eventually, the months and days of waiting were over. Alessia packed her things, said goodbye to her family and friends and flew off on an unforgettable adventure.

NORTH CAROLINA TAR HEELS

As an incredibly talented athlete, Alessia had multiple options when she decided to move to the USA. However, there was one college that stood out above the rest.

★ ALESSIA RUSSO ★

Alessia chose to study at the University of North Carolina at Chapel Hill, an institution known for having one of the best athletics programmes in the entire country. The programme was known to produce successful professional athletes and sporting legends. Basketball player Michael Jordan studied and trained there, as well as one of the USA's most famous female football players, Mia Hamm. This was the place to be for a student who wanted to be one of the best in their chosen sport.

Alessia wasn't just arriving as a new student, but as a student on a scholarship. This is when a college offers to pay the student's tuition fees because of their outstanding abilities in academics or sport. Alessia had travelled a long way from home and was nervous about being in a new place with new people, but there was no need to worry. She quickly learnt to love the lifestyle of a college athlete; everything had been arranged for her to play and develop to the best of her abilities. She was put in complete control. It was up to her to decide how much effort and determination she put into matches, studying and training.

It also helped that Alessia wasn't arriving on her own. A fellow footballer from England, who she had played with at youth camps, was joining her. Lotte Wubben-Moy was Alessia's roommate for the first year, and the two close friends helped each other navigate this new world that had opened up to them. Alessia didn't feel like she had to go through it all alone, because she had someone who was going through the same changes in life as she was.

During Alessia's first year, known in the US as a student's freshman year, she excelled in her own and the college's expectations of her. At this stage, Alessia played for the North Carolina Tar Heels as a winger, but that didn't stop her from getting on the scoresheet. She scored nine goals, making her the team's leading goalscorer. This was an exceptional feat for a player only at the beginning of their college career.

⭐ ALESSIA RUSSO ⭐

Alessia played her part in helping the team win the 2017 ACC Women's Soccer Tournament, defeating Duke University 1-0 in the competition's final. Alessia was named as the MVP for the match, which means 'most valuable player'. Alessia also earned a tremendous number of personal awards as her first season came to a close. She was named as the co-ACC Freshman of the Year, and she was added to the ACC All-Freshman team selection and United Soccer Coaches All-East Region selection. Adding to this, she was also celebrated by her own college as the best female newcomer in the athletics programme. It was fair to say that Alessia's freshman campaign was a hit.

Alessia returned home to England after finishing her first year of college. She reconnected with family and friends, before flying back out to continue her degree. She unfortunately missed the postseason with a broken leg, but Alessia wasn't going to let the injury set her back. After her body had healed, there was still enough time left in the season for Alessia to make an impact during her second year.

When she was back to full health, Alessia was unstoppable for the North Carolina Tar Heels. She played her part in helping the team win the regular season title for the first time since 2008. Alessia scored six goals in total, making her the team's joint-leading goalscorer. She also received more personal awards at the end of her second campaign. She was the first footballer from her college to be named in the United Soccer Coaches first team All-America selection since Crystal Dunn in 2013, and she was named as the ACC Offensive Player of the Year. She returned home to England with a heavy suitcase full of awards!

7
FOURTH YEAR

Alessia's pattern of success continued into her third year with the North Carolina Tar Heels. She helped the team defend their regular season title and win the 2019 ACC Women's Soccer Tournament. It was during this season that Alessia changed her position from midfield to centre forward, playing at the top of the pitch as an all-out attacker. Yet again, Alessia was the team's leading goalscorer with thirteen goals, and she picked up more awards. And for a second time, she was named in the United Soccer Coaches first team All-America selection and as the ACC Tournament MVP.

All signs pointed towards Alessia continuing this trend into her fourth year of college; she was expected to complete her degree and continue to dominate the world of college football. However, something entirely out of her control stopped that from happening. At the same time that Alessia arrived in the US to start her final year, COVID-19 shattered everyone's plans into a million pieces. The world everyone thought they knew turned into something else entirely.

Afraid that she wouldn't be able to leave the US if there was a lockdown, Alessia followed her parents' advice and flew back to England to be with her family. She was able to do this just in time – before most countries across the world began nationwide lockdowns. In a matter of weeks, Alessia's future had changed from playing matches in front of roaring fans to spending her days confined in a house with only her family for company.

As a family girl, this wasn't something Alessia hated. But she greatly missed the football matches she was never going to play and the memories she could have made with her friends over in the US. She waited for the pandemic to come to an end, but it dragged on and on with no one knowing when it might end.

Finally, after months of waiting, Alessia was allowed to travel back to college. However, things did not turn out as she had hoped on her arrival. Even though regular life had partially resumed, there were still many limits and protections in place. It was decided that the matches and students' education would continue during the final year, but the football teams would only play friendlies.

There would be no more competitions. Alessia loved to compete, so she had an incredibly difficult decision to make. She had caught the eye of the coaches from the England national team, and the last thing she wanted was for that momentum to stop. Women's football in England had resumed, albeit without fans in attendance, and competitive football was back in play. Alessia knew that she would be able to find a club to join back home. But that would mean having to close the door on her college experience and say goodbye to so many good friends and coaches. Once again, Alessia had reached a decisive moment in her career.

Alessia wanted to ensure her decision was the best one for her, so she took her time and asked everyone around her for their advice. The pieces of the puzzle started to fit together to form a picture, and soon she had decided what she wanted to do. It was time for Alessia to come back home. Her coaches and friends had recommended it, and Alessia knew deep down that it was the right decision. Word was put out to Women's Super League clubs that

★ **FOOTBALL RISING STARS** ★

Alessia was now available, and it didn't take long for offers to arrive. But one offer blew all the others away. One that Alessia felt she simply couldn't refuse. To play for the team she had supported as a child was her dream. It was a team that her grandfather, father and brothers all supported. Alessia was going to play for Manchester United.

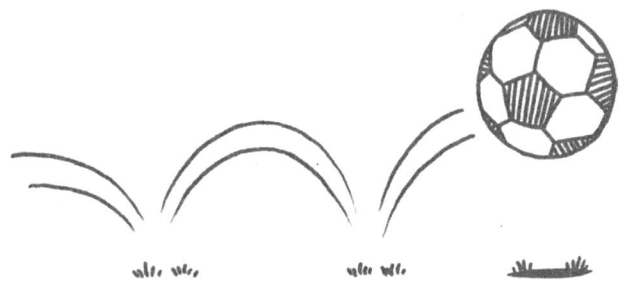

8

MANCHESTER UNITED: THE RED DEVILS

It all happened in the space of two weeks. In no time at all, Alessia had said goodbye to all of her friends at the University of North Carolina at Chapel Hill and had returned to

England. But it was not the England she was familiar with; Alessia was moving up north, to the city of Manchester, where she had signed her first ever professional football contract. It was all a blur, and Alessia was hardly aware of what to do with herself half of the time. Yet it was an exciting time that Alessia could appreciate after it had happened. She had realised her dream. Alessia was now a professional football player for a club in the top division of English football. And not only

that, it was the club that her family had supported for generations. The time for college football was over. This was the real deal.

It helped that Alessia knew some of the players at Manchester United. She had played with the tricky winger Ella Toone at her England youth camps, and the pair had quickly become best friends. They trained together each day at Manchester United and could often be seen giggling and joking with one another. They filled the training centre with laughter everywhere they went.

★ FOOTBALL RISING STARS ★

Only three days after signing, Alessia made her debut for Manchester United. She came onto the pitch as a half-time substitute in a 2-5 away victory against Birmingham City. Alessia didn't score on her debut, but she did get an assist for one of the goals. It didn't take her long to score her first goal for the club – just one match later. Alessia got herself on the scoresheet in a 3-0 match against Brighton & Hove Albion. Not long after, she scored her second and third goal for Manchester

United in a 2-4 away victory against West Ham United. But Alessia's goalscoring momentum was cruelly halted when she injured herself in a training session. She managed to tear her hamstring, and this injury kept her off the pitch for the remainder of the season. The tear was so bad that Alessia had to have reconstructive surgery to help her heal. Having gone through injuries before, Alessia knew how to handle the disappointment. With a good network around her and a strong mindset, she knew that she could get through this hardship.

⭐ FOOTBALL RISING STARS ⭐

By the time the 2021/2022 Women's Super League campaign came around, Alessia was ready to get back into action. She had spent far too long on the sidelines and was going to treasure every minute and opportunity on the pitch. During that season, Alessia made thirty appearances for the club in the league and domestic cups. She scored an impressive eleven goals in all competitions and helped her team finish fourth in the league. Fans had been back in attendance that season, so Alessia got to play in front of roaring crowds again. The women's team even played a match at the club's Old Trafford stadium in front of 20,241 fans. The previous year, the match had been played there with no fans in attendance. It was a dream come true for Alessia to walk out onto the pitch, where many of her childhood heroes had once played. And not only that, Alessia scored two of her team's goals that day in a 3-1 victory against Everton.

Alessia's time at Manchester United may not have started smoothly, but she had dealt with the pressure and

brought herself back from a serious injury. Alessia had proven herself as one of the best strikers not just in the league, but in the country. Her decision had paid off, and there were still many exciting achievements and opportunities around the corner.

9
ENGLAND DEBUT

Although Alessia had moved away to the US for college, she had always been on the radar of the England national team. She had played for their youth teams and had continued to do so throughout her developing career. While she was at college in the US, she'd received a text message from Phil Neville, England's manager at the time, inviting her to join the England national team. Alessia had been in the middle of a Geology class when she'd sneakily looked down at her phone. She was amazed that the England manager had messaged her. After class, Alessia had a phone call with Neville. He explained that she was being called up as a training player, not as a squad member, but Alessia could hardly contain her excitement. On that day, it was fair to say that she didn't attend any more of her college lessons. She was far too busy calling her family and friends to tell them the good news.

Alessia joined the team, with the matches conveniently taking place in the US as part of the SheBelieves Cup, and ended up being added to the primary squad due to an injury to Lucy Bronze. Alessia finally had a shot at making her debut. Even though the tournament didn't go England's way, it was still an incredible experience for Alessia to learn and play with some of the world's best. It was a testament to her professionalism that Neville brought Alessia on for her England debut in the final match of the tournament. England lost the match 1-0 to Spain, but Alessia felt immense pride while wearing the England shirt on the pitch, playing in front of over 10,000 fans in the Toyota Stadium in Texas. This was a feeling that she loved and wanted to experience over and over again.

Alessia had clearly impressed management, because she was invited to join England at future

camps and friendlies. By this time, she had joined Manchester United. After she returned from her hamstring injury, it was time for Alessia to be integrated back into the national team.

On the 30th of November 2021, England played against Latvia in a qualifying match for the 2023 World Cup. Both the team and Alessia enjoyed a record-breaking day. England won the match by an astonishing 20-0 scoreline, which broke a national record for their largest victory in a senior international football match. Alessia achieved a personal record too, scoring a hat-trick in the space of only eleven minutes. It was the fastest hat-trick scored by any England player in history. This England team appeared unstoppable, and Alessia was loving every moment with the side. But an important tournament was on the horizon. England would be competing in the UEFA Women's Euro 2022, a major international tournament that England were

★ ALESSIA RUSSO ★

hosting. There were so many talented players, and all of them wanted to be included. England's new manager Sarina Wiegman had a tough choice to make. She had to decide who to name in the squad and who to leave out. Alessia had been playing well for her club and country, but she had never been to a major international tournament before, so she would be viewed as an inexperienced player. As the days passed and the squad announcement day approached, Alessia concentrated all her efforts on playing well (and crossed her fingers). She trained and played to the best of her ability, hoping that it was enough to be named in the twenty-three player England squad.

10
EURO 2022

The summer of 2022 had arrived. Now that their regular seasons had come to a close, it was a time when most football players were planning their next holiday to warm and exotic locations. But that was not what Alessia was doing. Her summer plans had been put on hold and all she could do was closely watch her phone. She was waiting for a call, a text or a sign – anything to let her know whether she had been selected.

The days slowly passed by, and then it finally came. Alessia had been selected for the England squad! She was going to take part in her first ever major international tournament. Now Alessia's nerves switched from waiting to know if she had been picked in the squad to wanting to play her best at the tournament! Her nerves were mixed with excitement and adrenaline. She was one of the lucky few who had been picked to play in a home tournament, which was a once in a lifetime opportunity for a professional football player.

Alessia packed her things and joined the rest of the team at the St. George's Park National Football Centre, a state-of-the-art complex built to aid all levels of England football teams – whether women's or men's – to perform to the best of their ability. There was an incredible feel-good factor around the place.

★ **FOOTBALL RISING STARS** ★

The sun was shining, and the players were ready to put the work in to earn a spot in the starting lineup. There was something different about this tournament to previous competitions. The women's game in England had been steadily gathering momentum over the last few years, with matches getting more TV coverage and players finally starting to get the attention that they deserved. For the first time, the players were becoming celebrities – not just footballers.

★ ALESSIA RUSSO ★

The majority of the country eagerly awaited the start of the tournament, ready to cheer on the Lionesses in the competition.

England had been placed in Group A alongside Austria, Norway and Northern Ireland. It was a group that many hoped and expected England to progress from. These expectations could have easily transformed into pressure, but these England players were ready for the fight. They had created a feeling of togetherness and hope that had spread across the entire country.

★★ FOOTBALL RISING STARS ★★

As hosts, England would be kicking off the tournament. The first match took place on the 6th of July 2022, at a stadium that Alessia knew very well: England were playing against Austria at Old Trafford.

Despite Alessia's hard work in training, she was named on the bench for the opening match. Instead, Wiegman opted to play the experienced Ellen White in attack for the team. White had a legendary status in the squad as a striker, and she had scored over fifty goals for her country. Alessia watched on in amazement as her team walked out of the tunnel and onto the pitch. More than 68,000 fans had come to watch the match, which was a record-breaking crowd for a European Women's Championship game. The fans cheered and clapped as the team walked onto the famous turf. The players allowed themselves a handful of seconds to take in the wonder and spectacle of the moment. But they couldn't allow themselves too long. This team had a job to do and they needed to focus on their task.

In a tight game, England were able to get the tournament off to a winning start. Beth Mead scored the only goal of the match and England won 1-0. Alessia was brought onto the pitch as a substitute, and she helped her team close out the match and start the competition with three points.

England carried this momentum into the rest of the tournament, claiming an astonishing 8-0 victory

★ ALESSIA RUSSO ★

against Norway in their second match. It was in this match that Alessia scored her first major international goal. The team then closed out the group with a 0-5 victory against Northern Ireland. Alessia scored two of England's goals in that match, helping her country finish the group stage of the tournament in style. England and Alessia had progressed to the knock-out rounds of the tournament, where they would be competing against the best football players in Europe.

★ FOOTBALL RISING STARS ★

Would Alessia and England be able to continue their momentum?

11

THE RUSSO

England were drawn against Spain for a tough quarter-final. England endured a big scare during this match, as Spain scored the first goal of the game. But with their togetherness and courage, the team were able to fight back. England scored a late equaliser in the 84th minute, thanks to Alessia's best friend Toone. The winger was able to fire the ball into the back of the net, following a cushioned header from Alessia, and keep England's hopes of progressing further in the tournament alive. Neither side were able to find a winner in regular time, so the match was decided during extra time.

After being brought onto the pitch in the second half, Alessia was doing everything she could to push her team forwards. In the 96th minute,

⋆✦ ALESSIA RUSSO ✦⋆

Keira Walsh fed a pass to Georgia Stanway. The tenacious midfielder sent the entire stadium into a frenzy as she unleashed a strike from long-range. The Spanish goalkeeper could do nothing as the ball thwacked into the back of the net. England had taken the lead! Alessia and England held onto their position and were able to emerge victorious from a tough match. Even though it had been the team's hardest match to date, they had gotten past this obstacle together.

★ FOOTBALL RISING STARS ★

 England's next opponents were Sweden. The team needed to come together once more in order to make it to the final game of the competition and compete for the chance to be crowned as tournament winners. While Alessia wasn't starting matches, she was getting plenty of game time. Wiegman had made a tactical plan, and it was working wonders in the tournament so far. She would start the match with some of the more experienced players such as White, Mead and Fran Kirby, before

★ ALESSIA RUSSO ★

looking towards Alessia, Toone and Chloe Kelly (her younger impact players) in the latter stages of games. Wiegman continued this trend into the semi-final and it worked a treat.

England took the lead in the first half, thanks to goals from Mead and Bronze, giving England a 2-0 advantage at half time. When Alessia was brought onto the pitch in the second half, the fans in the stadium stood up to applaud her. Alessia had been a threat throughout the tournament and the fans were excited to see her play again. And in this second half, Alessia carried out an attack that would live up to this promise. She would be part of a goal that would go down as one of the best goals of the tournament.

In the 68th minute, Walsh played a precise through ball into the Swedish penalty box. Kirby ran onto the pass and looked up. The box was filled with Swedish defenders, but there was also a Lioness prowling near the edge of it. Kirby passed the ball back to Alessia, and she shot at

ALESSIA RUSSO

goal. The strike arrowed forward and hit the goalkeeper. It appeared that the chance was gone as the ball rebounded to the left. Alessia fought for control of the ball, with two defenders by her side and the goalkeeper in close company. But in a moment of quick thinking, and with an exceptional effort, Alessia shocked not only everyone in the stadium, but herself too. With her striker's instinct, knowing the ball was behind her, Alessia had to do something different. She had no choice but to move *away* from the goal and then backheel the ball. Amazingly, it shot past the two defenders behind her, slipped through the legs of the goalkeeper and rolled over the line! Alessia immediately threw her arms in the air in celebration and ran to the corner to celebrate with her teammates. No one could quite believe what they had just seen. Alessia had scored an incredible goal in one of the biggest games of her life. Even a handful of Swedish fans could do nothing but applaud the brilliance of the goal.

★ ALESSIA RUSSO ★

Sometimes, a move is just so good that everyone can appreciate it – no matter which team you're following.

Kirby added a fourth goal in the 75th minute, and England won the match 4-0. This left just one more hurdle to overcome. Alessia and England had made it to the final!

12
THE FINAL

All of Alessia and England's hard work had paid off. The team had made it to the final of the competition and were within touching distance of the trophy. But in order to claim it they needed to defeat a defiant German side. Germany were tough footballing opponents that had the same dreams as England. But despite both teams' recent successes, at the end of the day there was only going to be one winner.

The England team emerged from the Wembley tunnel to applause and cheers. The Lionesses were being cheered on by a record-breaking 87,192 fans in the stadium and by millions who were watching at home on their TVs. It was the event of the summer and no one was going to miss a minute.

As usual for the tournament, Alessia was starting the match on the

 bench. But she was ready. Alessia was going to do everything she could to help her team get through this final and reach heights never seen before by the country.

The first half was a cagey affair. While both sides desperately wanted to win the match, they both also didn't want to lose it. And so, the players were a little more cautious than usual, trying to eliminate any mistakes from their game in such a high-pressure environment. The teams were level at half-time, with neither side scoring a goal, but Wiegman was far from worried. Her team had been playing well, and she still had a trick up her sleeve that had come in useful throughout the entire tournament. It was time to use her impact players on the substitutes bench.

Early in the second half, Alessia and Toone were brought into the match. The two close friends were delighted to be brought into a match in a major international final only a few seconds apart. It was this togetherness and ability that started to cause concern for Germany. Alessia's impressive hold-up play and Toone's darting runs were turning the tide.

In the 62nd minute, Walsh played an incredible long-range pass over the German defence. Toone, full of energy since coming on, chased after the ball. The tiring German defenders were unable to keep up with her. Toone brought the ball under her control. As the German goalkeeper, Merle Frohms, rushed out to meet her, Toone made her decision. She lofted the ball over Frohms and it appeared to fall back down to earth in slow motion. Was it going over? Would it hit the crossbar and bounce out? No, the ball dropped perfectly and landed in the back of the net. England had the lead! They were winning in the final!

Toone raced off to celebrate as Wembley turned from a crowd of nervous fans into thousands of cheering and smiling faces. Everyone in the stadium rose to their feet and cheered for the Lionesses as they took the lead. But the game was far from won, as there were still many minutes of football yet to be played.

Germany proved this in the 79th minute. Lina Magull fired in an equaliser to bring the scores level. England's party atmosphere had been dampened but it had not been extinguished. Alessia and the team came together – they knew they could still do this. This wasn't a setback that would stop them, just a note in a story that they could still control.

Neither side could win the match

during regular time, and the game now had to be settled in extra time.  If the fans in the stadium weren't nervous before, they certainly were now. Everyone was sitting on the edges of their seats, keeping their fingers crossed, hoping that England could get over the line.

In the 110th minute, England had earned a corner. Alessia and her teammates jostled with German defenders for ground. Lauren Hemp swung the ball into the box and Alessia jumped for it, alongside a group of defenders and attackers. The ball went past her, but it hit Bronze and bounced into the box. Alessia was unable to go after the loose ball, because one of the German defenders had crashed into her. She felt a sudden pain shoot through her as the studs on the German player's boot, combined with her full weight, landed on Alessia's foot. She fell to the ground with no idea what was going on behind her.

Amid the chaos in the box, Kelly was able to react first and prodded the ball into the back of the net, sending the entire stadium into delirium as England took the lead once more. Alessia was one of the only people in the stadium, and perhaps in the country, who hadn't seen it. Hearing the roars, Alessia jumped up off the ground and ran to celebrate. Slowly piecing together what had happened, the pain in Alessia's foot almost started to disappear. All she could feel was pure jubilation and the excitement of being in the lead again, and of being so close to winning the match.

In the remaining minutes, Germany tried their best to find an equaliser. But Alessia and her teammates were not going to let this lead slip. The German coaches wanted to get a message to their players, so they wrote some tactical information on a piece of paper and passed it onto the pitch. As an opposition player was reading it, Alessia peeked over their shoulder to see what it said. Fortunately, it wasn't in German. Instead, it was a tactical drawing indicating a positional change. Everyone in the stadium laughed as they watched Alessia and the team truly do anything to keep hold of their advantage and win the match.

A few minutes later, the referee finally blew the whistle and the players could celebrate. Many of them burst into tears on the pitch or simply fell to the ground as they realised the scope of what they had just achieved. Alessia and this team had just won the Euros! During the celebrations, the pitch was covered in confetti and each player received a medal to treasure and hold for the rest of their lives. This team had just written itself into the history books of English football forever. For now, the time for seriousness and hard work was over. It was time to party!

13

THE RUMOUR MILL

The Lionesses were hailed as heroes. They had achieved a historical feat and deserved all of the praise they received. Alessia celebrated with the team, and as one of the stars of the tournament she was also invited to multiple private interviews.

Her performance in the Euros had made her a footballing sensation, and TV stations and media outlets  wanted to discover more about England's star striker. This period was a whirlwind for Alessia, but it was one filled with smiles and happiness. With each passing day, the reality of what she had achieved was setting in. Alessia was a Euros winner!

After a summer of celebration, it was finally time for the 2022/2023 Women's Super League to start. Alessia, eager as ever, was ready to compete in a tough season to help Manchester United finish high in the table. With Alessia's help, Manchester United managed to finish in second place in the league, narrowly missing out on first place by finishing two points behind Chelsea. Throughout the season Alessia scored thirteen goals for the side, making her the club's top goalscorer across the entire campaign. Alessia's top performances as one of the best strikers in the league were not going unnoticed. Halfway through the season, Arsenal made a record-breaking bid of £500,000 to sign Alessia. Manchester United did not want to sell their star striker to a rival and declined the offer. But while this offer was not accepted, it started a series of events that would greatly affect Alessia's next steps.

Her contract with Manchester United was in its final year, so Alessia would either need to sign a new deal with the club or consider a move elsewhere. Since she was such an important player, Manchester United offered Alessia new contracts on improved terms. But as someone fond of

adventure, Alessia started to consider what life would be like at a new club. Although she had enjoyed her time at Manchester United, perhaps it was time for her to write a new chapter, to push herself further in a new environment with different coaches, teammates and surroundings. But this was not a choice to be taken lightly. While there were many positives to be earned from a move, there were also many things that she would miss. She would miss playing with her close friends, her coaches and all of the supportive fans who had cheered her on during her time at the club.

Alessia had a decision to make and it was far from a simple one. She had a chance to control her future and choose where she would be playing her football next. As a professional with a limited amount of playing years in her career, it was a chance for Alessia to set herself up for the future and make sure that she received what she deserved as one of the best in the game.

14
ALESSIA'S CHOICE

Alessia now finds herself in a completely different world to the one she grew up in. Women's football used to be seen as a sidenote rather than the main event, but those days are over. Over the course of one summer, a country and perhaps even the world started to realise the truth. That women's football is an incredible sport filled with talented stars, athletes and personalities. It is a sport that is here to stay and deserves to be watched and enjoyed by millions across the globe.

As a result of her success, Alessia is a recognisable celebrity. She has earned multiple deals with large name brands who want to sponsor her and be associated with her talent and endearing personality. She truly has come so far from her time playing football on the sidelines of her brothers' matches, and from her

★ ALESSIA RUSSO ★

days learning, playing and enjoying her football at West Farleigh and Bearsted. Alessia had found her feet at Manchester United and made a name for herself, both at club level and on the international stage. But now that her contract has reached its end, Alessia has made a decision. It's time for her to pursue a new opportunity. Alessia has returned south, moving closer to her roots, and signed for Arsenal. Her announcement was met with an overwhelming response of excitement and joy from Arsenal fans. Their club had signed one of

the best footballers in England, so their enthusiasm wasn't misplaced. The club posted numerous videos on social media revealing their new star player to the world.

Over the summer of 2023, Alessia played her part in an inspiring and successful World Cup campaign. With Alessia's help, England progressed to the final of the competition. Progressing further than thirty other countries and being one of the last two teams in the tournament is an impressive feat. However, a World Cup win for England wasn't to be.

★ ALESSIA RUSSO ★

Despite her best efforts, Alessia couldn't help England over the line. Spain were victorious in the final and Alessia had to settle for a runners up medal.

Yet Alessia's tournament had been far from a waste. Alessia scored her first ever World Cup goal in the group stages, opening the scoring in a 6-1 victory over Group D opponents China. Alessia also scored the winner in a hard-fought contest with Colombia in the round of 16. Not to forget her heroic deciding goal in the semi-final, where England overcame the tournament co-hosts, Australia.

Alessia has built a habit of being the player her team can turn to when they need her most. No matter the pressure, or the enormity of the situation, Alessia can be depended upon. This quality is something that her country and professional clubs will always cherish. As the star from Maidstone, she has plenty of finals and deciding matches still ahead of her. Alessia's goals, kind nature and talent will keep fans smiling for years to come.